The Outrageous 19th

JOY OF GOLF

by
Les Arnett

Thanks to Alex Kelly, Graham Brock and Joe Monro

This book was first published under the title of
Rude Golf for Beginners
and has been redesigned for
The Outrageous 19th Group

Published by
Outrageous 19th Limited 2007

Produced by
Jigsaw Print and Production Limited

First Published 1996

Reprinted 1998, 2000

ISBN 978-0-9555601-0-1

CONTENTS

Chapter I

PLAYING AROUND
- A COURSE TRADITION

IN THE BEGINNING - Even the first hole was a temptation

HISTORICAL ROOTS

The Rude Golf Society has been around as long as the game itself. In some ways its traditions pre-dates golf, as some of our founder members belonged to the oldest professional occupation known to man. These old pros have made sure that their skills and expertise have been passed on to the club pros of today.

The Rude Golf Society Pro shop makes good use of this ancient knowledge and are experts in easing the members' frustrations by offering their services orally, showing better grips and techniques and being on hand for relief in their clinics.

The oldest record of the Rude Golf Society dates from 1744. This was an entry in an Edinburgh Gentleman's Diary, a Captain Jock Straps – he was recounting an incident he witnessed when a gentleman was seen playing with a brassie on a Scottish links. "After some time thrashing about in the rough the man emerged in some disarray, he must have met with some kind of accident as he was cradling his shaft and shouting I think I have a goner here."

After this unfortunate encounter the first set of rules for the Rude Golf Society were drawn up; safety play being paramount. The oldest surviving rule which is still in use today is Rule 1.25: "Neither Ditch nor Dike or Scholar holes shall be accounted a hazard", which only goes to show how liberal the society has always been.

Since the Rude Golf Society sunk their first putt and holed out successfully they have had lady players all with equal rights.

In fact some of our females have dominated many male members and have been very strict in upholding the rules, administering severe punishments to the naughtiest offenders.

During the Victorian period the Rude Golf Society had its first female Vice-Captain Miss Spankhurt. Up until then the Society had gone through many Lady Pros, but she introduced male pros into the clubs. Her belief was, although women could play around with members, coaching was all too brief, with little follow through and often a limp response after the first hole. She wanted her girls to experience the full satisfaction of a hole in one and to distinguish a short shaft from an over sized head.

The gentlemen players were not too keen on the introduction of male pros and many boycotted the pro shops although there was a small number of chaps who secretly approved and continued to visit the club pros through a small entrance at the rear. This is where the golfing term "Bandits" is first thought to have originated. After a short turbulent period it was decided to introduce visiting pros to satisfy all camps.

During the war years the male membership dropped off (this had happened many years earlier during the plague but a strong course of penicillin seemed to cure this). Many ladies took on the role of male members and a tradition of female foursomes began. This started a controversy over the role of artificial aids. The Rules Committee decided that in certain circumstances, two ladies or more playing with each other, may use shaft extensions to allow them to get the necessary length when playing off of the male teeing position. There has always been a concession to

HADRIAN'S BALL - The first invasion of overseas players took up the eagle as a lucky omen

ladies playing with themselves as long as they allow others to play through.

When the Americans entered the war, they supplied a much needed boost to the flagging membership. This was the start of the American branch of the Rude Golf Society. They even took the quaint old English war time saying of "Keep your pecker up" as their motto.

This was also the time of the first overseas Vice-Captain, the Bostonian Johnny Fitzanybody, closely followed by the Mexican, Juan Size.

Now the Rude Golf Society is world wide and course golf is on the increase, we arrange Pro-Am tournaments in many countries.

Exchange partner evenings have proved very popular where a great deal of intercourse takes part and players are encouraged to display their equipment.

Techniques and score cards are usually the subjects of debate. The Rude Golf Society is open to all whether you wish to be a course observer or have the stamina to play 36 holes in a day. **Our President's statement is:** *"Size and ability count for nothing, as long as our members stand proud and erect, it's how we play the game."*

President elect: **Ivor Smallcock.**

Chapter II

VICE CAPTAINS AND COURSE PROS

COURSE POSITIONS

Unlike ordinary golf clubs and societies the Rude Golf Society has no captain, only a vice-captain. This prestigious honour is bestowed upon long standing members who have served the players or officers of the committee. They will also would have been seen doing their duty when called upon.

This post is open to ladies but a slightly different criterion may apply. All applicants have to be personally vetted by the committee.

The course pro is the only paid employee of the society, this is a time honoured custom. But all assistant or visiting pros rely on gratuities and the generosity of their clients. Private lessons are a matter of negotiation depending on one-to-one or group participation.

Regular clinics are held on a weekly basis where players' equipment can be examined free of charge. Small problems can be sorted out on the spot.

All players are advised to take out insurance against accidents or injury. The committee ask members not to play around whilst undergoing treatment.

RULES OF THE GAME - Playing the same hole time and time again makes it difficult for other players to have a go.

MOSSY HOLLOWS PRESENT VICE-CAPTAIN
DREW PEACOCK

Mr Drew Peacock has been Vice-Captain at the Rude Golf Society UK Headquarters, Mossy Hollow Golf Club for the past five years.

Unlike most Golf Societies and clubs our elected members may stand as many times as their stamina allows. Although entrants for his seat are offered annually so far there have been no takers and his passage remains unblocked for a further term.

Mr Peacock first took up Rude Golf some 15 years ago, but he has been a lifelong player with the Oddfellows Society, where he also held a position of service. In all his years with the Oddfellows he never lacked support and many members have been happy to stand behind him.

At the start of Drew Peacock's working life he joined the navy, since coming out he has spent most of his career in drapery and has travelled in ladies' underwear for the last ten years. With this rag trade background he heads the Dress Code Committee and deals with all queries. Mr Peacock believes in familiarity and insists on handling all male members personally. He usually passes on the female players' demands to two assistants who are from Eastern Europe, a small Czech with a tall Pole, although he does help out on occasions just to keep his finger in.

MOSSY HOLLOW'S PRESENT PRO
RUSTY CRACK

Miss Crack has enjoyed her position as course pro for more years than she cares to remember.

Through this period she has introduced many young talented assistants to help her with her ever-popular clinic. Although her participation is mainly oral now, she still likes to keep astride any new techniques that raise their head.

Also as a rule of the club, any virgin players have to be assessed by her before being allowed to play a round with the members. Miss Crack tends to specialise in one-to-one coaching, in fact she has only taken on two group sessions before, once with the Household Cavalry and once with the American Navy.

She found having so many balls around the hole very confusing and didn't know if she was coming or going.
There seemed to be seamen everywhere and it was really more than she could swallow.

Since this unfortunate incident, group coaching is limited to three members per pro or four on a staggered arrangement as long as they do not all come together.

ROLL OF HONOUR – MOSSY HOLLOW GOLF CLUB

Below is our role of honour from the United Kingdom Rude Golf Society Headquarters, Mossy Hollow Golf Club.

Vice-Captains

Ginger Pecker

Phil John Thomas

Johnny Fitzanybody

Juan Size

Miss A. Spankhurt

Tiny Hampton

Red Gonads

Curly Pubes

Sean Pubes

Arthur Bollock

Paul Dickov

Dusty Klinker

Manny Cummings

Ivor Bigun

Fila MacOkie

Pros

Fanny Hare

Ema Royds

Rosie Buttocks

Gay Cottagar

Phil McAvity

Andy Jobe

Queeny Mincing

Scarlet Beveur

Ruby Quims

Ida Crabes

Mini Hooters

Maxie Juggs

Oraly Knoblick

Di Reara

Pat MacLitorus

A SLICED BALL - Lack of concetration at the address can lead you to drop goolie - remember to keep your eye on the ball.

Chapter III

ON THE TEE

THE TEE

The teeing ground is a very important area within the game of Rude Golf. Where a player places his balls can make or break a narrow bushy entry. The etiquette of who goes first or the condition of your equipment must be learned and adhered to.

Preparation is the key to a relaxing game. Make sure you have pre-booked with the course pro before inserting your peg.

Chancing your luck and hoping you can slip in behind someone else while they are still playing the hole can get you into trouble. Intercourse between players and caddies while waiting at the tee should be kept to a minimum, as it may cause excessive strain on a player who needs to concentrate to complete his motion.

The following rules and tips will help you with your knee trembles and give you the confidence to lie back and take whatever comes.

THE HONOUR

The honour is the term used for the privilege of having the first stroke on a virgin round. Usually the player with the least experience or the worst scorer goes first, he is looked upon as someone who would benefit from being allowed to screw in his peg before the others.

For the more experienced players, the handicapping system would come into play. (See Rude Golf Handicaps.) But if all handicaps are equal the players are expected to toss for the honour. Assistance with the toss may be offered from partners or caddies. The Vice-Captain is always willing to lend a hand.

ADDRESSING THE BALL

The address is the term for the position taken up before playing with your balls. Once you have decided who is going first, perhaps after a quick toss, your positioning becomes very important.

The correct placement of the player's balls are critical at the address. It is often wise to take a long look up the fairway and contemplate your first stroke. Most players like to achieve a vertical shaft. However we are not all built the same, what is comfortable for some may be painful for others.

Several of our greatest players have turned in a fantastic performance from a very limp swing which is barely ever upright. Also no two holes are ever the same so addressing to the left or right can sometimes make for a smoother stroke.

An open stance is always very popular with female players. With a wider fairway you may find you need to bring your legs closer together to stop the drive wandering off to the side. The tighter the action, the quicker the delivery. Although the use of a oversized driver will mean you need to get further back from the balls and probably adopt a splayed position.

HAVING THE HONOUR - The privilege of going first on a virgin hole. No need for a quick toss, get straight into inserting your peg.

TIPS FOR THE ADDRESS

1. At the address some players bend their knees to help their motion. The best way of achieving the correct position is to relax and imagine you are easing yourself down onto a very tall stool.

2. After selecting your tool take the best and most comfortable position. Try not to rush your shot, use a nice slow draw back. Balance and rhythm are the key.

3. The object of the stance is to get your various body parts into positions from which you can make the most effective use of your equipment, so your balls do not stray from the target.

4. Firmly plant your feet with knees slightly bent and both hands on the tool. Gently move your arms back and forth, cocking the wrists. Just let it happen naturally.

THE WAGGLE

To loosen up at the address, small waggles whilst holding the shaft can strengthen the fingers and keep the grip in place. This action gives you the feel of the wrists working and the swing of the head. Motion, momentum and gravity are major aspects of this technique, especially with female players. Excessive waggling can sometimes prove distracting to players.

LADIES TEES

Normally the ladies tees are directly in front of the male members.

Lady players have the option of playing off any tee, this is to accommodate females who prefer to play off a shorter length or with each other. Alternatively the longer the length the bigger the challenge and shaft extensions may help.

There is a concession to male players who prefer to play from the female positions. These may be members who swing both ways. They must clearly indicate the hole they are intending to play, as cross dressing can cause confusion.

TOPPING THE BALL

Players balls are said to have been topped when clean contact has not been made. Through a combination of a misalignment of the shaft and swinging back too early, the head can just clip the edge of the ball. Topping the balls are often the cause of much discomfort on the tee and can result in balls being deemed unfit for play or completely lost.

There is more than one way to top or slice a ball, remember always to stand well back when other members are about to complete their shot.

Rude Golf can be a dangerous sport and it is wise to concentrate when your balls are at risk. Unfortunate accidents can be avoided. Caddies should always check topped balls for damage.

COMING OFF THE SHOT

By getting the rhythm wrong and raising your body too early causing the head to rise prematurely is known as coming off the shot.

LOOSENING UP EASES THE ACTION - Excessive waggling may be a distration and cause a premature shoot.

THE LADIES' TEE - Although these tees are available, some ladies refer to play off the longer male peg.

Tips For On The Tee

Some of our less experienced players and especially the ladies find the opening strokes difficult. Although stiffness is to be expected, the longer equipment taken at the outset of a round is hard to handle when you're not warmed up. A painful experience can often be avoided by taking something smaller to start with, you can score just as well with a few shorter straight strokes delivered safely. These can be just as pleasurable as an uncontrollable lunge with the biggest tool.

Shanking . . . it's not always easy for the rude golfer to concentrate on his game with all that's going on around him. Whilst swinging off the tee, a small misalignment of the hands when cocking the wrists can result in a messy shank. This is when the shaft and ball collide during a stroke, a painful experience which can lead to the balls flying off at an acute angle.

There are many different ways the golfer can play off of the tee. Some of our more experienced caddies can offer excellent oral advice and like nothing better than to get their head round members' problems.

Caddies tip . . . "The strength of the blow governs the length of the shot."

Chapter IV

ON THE FAIRWAY

On The Fairway

The fairway is often treated with less respect than it deserves. Each one is different, they may twist and turn, undulate and roll. But you know all will end in the same way, whether the entry is tight or wide open, there is a tantalising lush area surrounding the final goal. So how do you get from your first stroke to your final penetration. There can be hidden dangers and hazards, many a member has lost more than one ball going from practice swing to hole. Always keep an eye out for slow players ahead, it's no good rushing your shot and coming upon them too early.

This sort of handiwork only antagonises everyone. Humps and deep gullies are all part of this game, the variations of shafts that can be used could have a novice open mouthed. Let's hope this section keeps you on the straight and narrow.

Awkward Lay

There are several ways a player's balls can be declared in an awkward lay. Trying to play in a restricted position can lead to the strangulation of your shot. It is true to say that taking a stroke while your balls are encumbered is a particularly brave thing to do, especially if you have entered a bit of rough only to find you've got entangled in a coarse matting or even clinkers.

The unusual state or condition of a player's balls when on the ground can constitute an awkward lie, particularly if in nettles, thistles or brambles. Alternatively an acute angle between the hand and shaft may also be said to be awkward.

FAIRWAY OR BUST - The best swingers in the Rude Golf Society are often exposed on the fairway

AWKWARD LAY / PUNCH SHOT

What may seem a very easy lay in the rough can be very deceiving. Make sure you read the right signs. A member can sometimes misconstrue the situation and decide that his partner or caddie does not mind him taking advantage of them by using excessive practice strokes. This can sometimes result in an unnecessary hook or punch shot.

DOG LEGS

This is a descriptive term often used on the fairway. It should not be used to describe a stance of another player, even if it seems appropriate.

Holes with a severe kink along their length are known as dog legs. This can make scoring difficult for the average player. Experienced Rude Golfers can position themselves to make their opening strokes shorter to nudge up to the bend. Then once a clear passage is visible the full length may be hit home. An additional hardship to be found on a dog leg is a blind shot to the green. Players should feel their way carefully to get abreast of the situation, before making a blind shot. Take care not to upset or interfere with other players or their equipment.

Hanging / Uphill / Downhill Lays

The Rude Golfer is used to many varied positions. In fact some players go out of their way to experiment with unusual lays, whether on top or below. A good shot from a difficult position can be most rewarding, especially if it has meant going down on it first.

Preferred Lie

Often the players have little choice in their lay. But should a better alternative be available, who can blame them for switching to something more desirable. Partners and caddies should not take offence.

Bunkers

When playing Rude Golf on the fairway players often find themselves in a hollow with raised lips. This cavity can be of indeterminable depth – or they find themselves in a bunker.

Strict bunker practice is taken very seriously by our players. Poor bunker technique may be punished by an excessive number of strokes being taken.

Special bunker classes are run by the society, as our members seem to spend much of their time thrashing about in the sand. After extracting yourself, check for sandy balls as such abrasives can damage the outerskin.

BUNKER PLAY
Too much time spent in a bunker can lead you to surrendering a game.

THE ROUGH - An open stance when going down in the rough can be uncomfortable. Careful not to get a nasty scrape.

On The Fairway

Rude Golfers with a cross to bear and a dictatorial nature find a good bunker a safe haven to work out their strategy before the final push towards the pole.

The first requirement in taking a fairway bunker shot is to check the lie. If it is anything less than clean and perfect, forget any fancy notions of distance. Just get in and get it out as quickly as possible.

Players can get disorientated in a bunker, keep your eye on the object in hand and try not to let your head bottom out.

Splashing

Some members like to put on a big show when stroking out of a bunker, the splash shot is coming out in style.

Small Pricks

When on the fairway and you come across a mossy mound where someone else has ploughed his furrow, just gently pat it down, don't be embarrassed at using a tiny tool, poke firmly around the edge.

Fairway maintenance is every player's problem, a series of small pricks can often make all the difference.

THE ROUGH

The rough is an area of both pain and pleasure. You may find yourself entangled in a bushy undergrowth, making it impossible to complete your follow through.

Sometimes really heavy tufts twist your shaft slightly to foul the stroke. This is when you dream of those well mown mounds. Many of our blue-blooded players like nothing better than picking up a rough lay and bonking their balls until they are physically exhausted.

OUT OF BOUNDS

Even in the Rude Golf Society certain areas are deemed out of bounds, depending on the player's preferences. All queries should be referred to Mr Drew Peacock, the Vice-Captain.

At certain periods or times of the month some holes may be out of bounds. Don't play a hole if a red warning flag is flying.

RAW SWINGERS - Novices may not see the need to protect their equipment, most old pros know excessive exposure may affect the delicate touch - that can be tough titty.

TIPS FOR ON THE FAIRWAY AND IN THE ROUGH

While playing through thick undergrowth make firmer strokes than normal, chopping thrusts with plenty of follow through are the only way to reach the intended target.

Wet conditions in deep rough can cause problems, a build up of moisture on the head can soon result in a squirting action. Be careful, this type of shot can run and run.

Treat extremely matted lies with extreme caution, you never are quite sure what you will find. After playing your stroke, clean all equipment immediately.

Know every hole you are likely to play, disorientation during the excitement of stroke play could lead to a member aiming and playing at the wrong hole. As well as the embarrassment of this kind of slip, rhythm is always lost and your partner starts to doubt your reliability. This can often happen when playing in bad light, playing from behind the hole and concentrating on not overshooting again. Beware! Play this kind of shot too often and rumours can make you an undesirable partner.

On The Fairway

Being "plugged" in a closely mown area can cause problems for the inexperienced. A more advanced position is called for. Bend the knees, play a firmer stroke. Usually a combination of sliding a firm grip down the shaft and holding the hands just behind the ball will help with the smooth stroke necessary for a tight lie.

Ball cleaners are positioned at various points around the course. Unlike other clubs, members of the Rude Golf Society usually have their balls cleaned for them, it has become a ritual. After every hole played the players' balls are lifted and inspected for dirt and other deposits found in the dimples, a quick lick and a rub with a fluffy towel is all that is normally required.

After a particularly mucky hole attention should also be paid to the little grooves running around the head of the club. This can lead to irritation later on after finding you get a bad result. Remember, nobody likes to play with dirty equipment.

Chapter V

ON THE GREEN

HOLDING THE POLE
Once you are on the green a player can ask his caddie to hold his pole.

On The Green

From teeing up your balls and looking longingly up the inviting fairway to standing shaft erect, ready for the final thrust, you have now found the G-spot, that soft lush area with its divine orifice.

All rude golfers dream of that wonderful moment of entry. It doesn't matter if you are a good or poor player, whether you have chosen the biggest tool available or been satisfied with something more manageable to get to this climax. You are now ready to sink that hole.

Holing out is probably the most frustrating part of the game. Having your balls so close yet so far from the hole can have you shaking with anticipation. Time should be taken before committing your shot, study the hole, don't be afraid of the distance between you and the hole – remember, length isn't everything.

Try to measure your length carefully, push too hard and you may slip up and overshoot. This will mean that you have to try and come back on yourself – a messy business.

THE GENTLE TOUCH

Once you have made your way to this hallowed ground the nature of the game changes. From the strength and passion needed for the approach strokes to one of subtlety and finesse where a player must adopt a more sensitive touch.

Finger tip control and a smooth movement is required; a quick hand jerk and the whole build up could be lost.

RUB OF THE GREEN

The rub of the green – or luck, plays an important part of any game. Whether playing in competition, say a foursome or playing with oneself, a good rub on the green can relieve built up frustration.

SIZE OF TOOL

In recent years some rude golfers have come on the green with abnormally large equipment. These long tools are often bragged about in the bar, but during actual play increased performance has not usually been reported. It is felt the use of such an appendage is for show or to make the opposition feel inadequate.

The rules committee have decided that when you are on the green, if you have to hold your tool halfway down the shaft and still be at arm's length from your balls, then your partner may claim the hole under the new intimidation rule.

BALLS OVERHANGING THE HOLE

Sometimes after making a stroke when holing out, your balls are left overhanging the hole. There may be a hush of anticipation as they quiver on the edge, but it is a mark of etiquette not to wait too long before making your final insertion. Finish it off and let someone else have their turn.

THE APRON

Within the Rude Golf Society the apron can be a very secretive part of a member's play. The grip is also unusual and only practised with others in the know. This type of play is restricted to male players. Whilst there are no females to beaver away in the lodge, ladies are often invited to participate on the fringes.

THE APRON ON THE RISE

Many members find it easy to hole out from the apron, and the challenge of a rising apron can sometimes prove more exciting. The more the apron rises the harder it gets, these situations may be something to bone up on.

THE LUCKY RUB - *Rude Golfers can be very superstitious, they often wish for a four leaf clover or a little goblin on the green.*

MARKING YOUR BALLS

When it is another player's turn to play and you are waiting, take the opportunity to lift your balls and inspect for damage. This is particularly important if your last shot could have damaged the outer skin, or where a shot played from a dirty lay could have left a deposit resulting in irritation later on.

HOLDING THE POLE

When members are ready to sink their putt it is quite acceptable for them to ask caddies to hold their poles for them. All our caddies are trained in this art. They find the best method is to grab the pole firmly and hold it just a few millimeters above the hole. This adds to the anticipation and makes the player concentrate. If a lengthy shot is achieved it is also acceptable for both player and caddie to be very vocal on final penetration. The cries of "Yes, Yes, Yes" are often heard.

LINING UP THE PUTT

With the caddie holding the pole, the player may take the opportunity to view the hole from several angles. It is not unknown for players to lie on the floor to get a look along the line of entry. In fact an in-depth study of the hole will help you understand what is required. Check for any debris and remove it – run your finger around the edge, just to make sure there is nothing to snag your balls on.

LICKING AROUND THE FRINGE

There are many ways to make a satisfactory approach. Some players are experts in playing delicately in the fringed areas, just around the main playing surface. With a little tickle and great finesse a reasonable result can be achieved. Although you may find you fail to come all the way and an extra bonk may be needed to obtain final satisfaction.

Others prefer to play the same lies with a gentle uplifting shot and a full follow through, this can also lead into a good running delivery – often trickling down the hole.

WHO GOES FIRST

Rude golf etiquette demands that the player with the longest shot usually goes first. This may seem unfair to someone who only requires a little poke, and indeed if it is only a couple of inches nobody should mind or notice if they come first.

If it is not your turn you can learn a lot by watching others. To see an opponent trying his hardest and ending up just licking around the edge of the hole can give you the confidence to use an opening line to obtain direct access to the hole, dropping your own shot in without undue effort. Although "oneupmanship" is accepted as normal within the confines of rude golf, two players trying to outdo one another and making a play for the same hole can lead to bad feeling or a fracas which may culminate in both players having sore heads in the morning.

SPECIALIST CLUBS

The green probably has more variations of equipment than any other part of the course. We have already covered elongated shafts, but there are weighted heads to give you a heavier dong on contact, also various ends set at angles and attachment to line up on the hole. Not all rude golfers need such elaborate devices, then again variety is the spice of life.

CONSIDERATE PLAY

Constant pounding of the balls onto a manicured surface can lead to damage occurring. Considerate players like to make sure any hard-hit hollows are eased back into shape so as not to inconvenience later play.

Particularly vulnerable areas are the delicate lips around the edge of the hole. These can be easily chafed when a player unintentionally puts his full weight down when reaching deeply down into the hole.

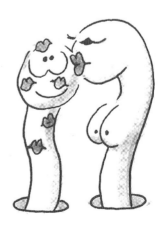

RISING APRON - Closely studying the inviting undulations around the fringe makes the choice of shaft a stiff one.

THE PUTTING LESSON - It is important when putting to focus on the back of the hole while keeping your eye on the lip.

SIZE OF THE HOLE

Holes are nearly always the same depth and circumference. However a nervy player, tightening up, can make the hole seem as small as a mousehole and almost impossible to get into while the confident player, swaggering towards the playing surface, sees an easy hole large enough to put your arm in. With a knowing smile he is in and his balls are rattling around. Down in one. After waving his scorecard he strolls off to find his next target to the applause of a knowledgeable crowd –
what a player.

GOLF BAGS

On the subject of golf bags, they are not to be had on the green. Apart from being unsightly, a lot of damage can be done when their heels are dug in before being dropped on their backs.

The Rude Golf Society Committee are trying to discourage humping old bags anywhere on the course . . . Leave your old bag at home, hire a new model from the proshop.

TIPS FOR ON THE GREEN

*Most lady players don't find it difficult to sink those hard 8"
putts. Men have been telling them 8" is the length of their little
pinky for years.*

*The pendulum technique is often used on the green to assist
the member to get straight into the hole. An upright shaft held
deftly between the fingers with one open eye aiming for just the
right spot shows the serious nature of this player. This technique
played to advantage allows the player to ride all the undulations
and hollows with confidence and to drop his shot effortlessly
into the welcoming cup.*

*Many players find the open stage of the green a too public place
to perform properly, blaming everything: from being rushed;
being watched; or strong wind; on their poor performance,
sometimes missing the hole completely. Lack of confidence must
be combated, as when you add up your final score, half of your
strokes take place on the green. One good tip on confidence
endorsed by our pro is not to aim for the front lip of the cup.
play a good firm stroke right to the back of the hole. Some
players like to close their eyes on making the stroke and instead
listen to the distinctive noise as their shots hit the target. It's
probably the best noise in the world.*

*Hardness can be a frustrating problem to a male rude golfer
early in the round, he only has to see a couple of bouncers
disappear off the back of the green to decide on playing a few
practice shots of a solitary nature whilst deciding how to make
the best approach.*

THE SLOW PLAYER - *Taking too much time on the green can lead to a blockage behind you.*

LOOSE FIT - Using old bags can lead to a loss of shaft and balls as their opening has usually gone slack and baggy.

On The Green

Care must be taken not to over practice before you play the hole, spontaneity is everything and over exertion can result in poor results when playing the real thing later on.

Unwelcome hardness on the green in those too hot moments can be combatted using the sprinkler system. A quick cold shower can be all that's needed to stop the frustration of a player over shooting early on. Great fun can be had with all sorts of sprinkler and some golden moments can be especially memorable.

Groups of players performing on the fairway are often out of sight of one another, in the rough, behind a tree, or trying to make a firm contact partly concealed in a welcoming hollow. The green however, is the natural stage for the proud member, the place where all players of a mixed foursome will come together, you will always be sure of an appreciative audience to enjoy your best shots.

The rigid techniques required for normal play can be dispensed with on the green. The general rule is: "If it feels good, and it works, go for it". Rude golfers often use these very public moments to display their latest techniques of play, often going through a complicated ritual before making their hopeful final stroke. Some golfers for example like to examine the hole from behind before they play. Getting a good close up of the unfamiliar humps and hollows can be very helpful when taking aim.

Chapter VI

COURSE BEHAVIOUR

THE ETHICS OF PLAYING AROUND

Within the Rude Golf Society we have a very liberal attitude as to behaviour when playing around. Most golf clubs are governed by the fourteens rule, we are certainly not that liberal. There are one or two exceptions around the world, but generally we keep to the sixteens rule.

The Rules Committee often sit to update their position on contentious matters such as artificial aids, inflatables, battery operated devices and new techniques in threesomes or fourplay.

There is a full rule book available from the pro shop. This contains not only the facts and in-depth explanations about course behaviour but also is fully illustrated. The pictures are very explicit and are extremely helpful to the new comer. Unfortunately the copies that were kept in the locker rooms have now been removed, because of the expense of replacing them daily. We found that members were boning up for an excessive length of time, sometimes causing a blockage in the facilities.

GROUP PLAY - Some players find the slightest distration too much to handle.

THE AIR SHOT

As in any game of golf an air shot is an unfortunate occurrence. Indeed a lot of players give a little grunt when loosening up, or even when they strain. It is wise to concentrate on the action as you may find it embarrassing to create a little puff of wind around your balls when trying to make contact.

There are players who have no regard for others and constantly drop one during their game. The caddies of these persistent gas bags should always be prepared, especially when the player gets ready to let rip off the tee. Although annoying, there are no rules to govern the strength of an air shot, it is regarded as unacceptable behaviour to have more than 3 air shots on the tee – especially with other players and their caddies in close attendance.

The air shot can also be used as a form of gamesmanship. Any minor distraction may completely put players off their swing. If an opponent is about to start his stroke, a few good air shots, just off the tee, rattled out one after the other may give you an edge and a whiff of success.

THE BARE LAY

There are various bare lays within rude golf, but this term is usually used in connection with the amount of foliage or lack of it up the fairway. These smooth areas can occur for several reasons. They may happen as part of a natural habitat, which has a thin or wispy covering, perhaps overplayed where too many members have been pounding away or a piece of rough that demands constant re-seeding. Sometimes a bald zone is by choice to clear unwanted growth, to ease access or treat infestation.

LOOSE IMPEDIMENTS

Loose impediments are a common hazard to rude golfers. Natural objects of any size or shape provided they are not still growing may be moved at the discretion of the player.

There are many loose lies to be found at Mossy Hollow. Remember you may pick-up and toss off any object whether it impedes play or not. Be careful when tugging at living objects as there are penalties for moving balls. If the obstruction is dead it can be pulled and played in the normal way. Although the Ethics Committee are looking into this as well as pulling dead and decaying matter. Exposing a buried lay is considered bad form.

STIFF COMPETITION - It can be frustrating watching another player make his shot, but the rule of not interfering while balls are in motion still applies.

COMPETITIONS

Competitions form an integral part of the Rude Golf Society. Our members enjoy the skins tournaments and four skins are a particular favourite with many of our ladies. Unfortunately some of our orthodox members feel they are penalised in this circumspect area.

In any golf club there is a large social element, getting to know more people interested in sport plays a big part. All members are different whether young, old, big, small, black or white, great fun can be had trying out new partners. It's no different for rude golfers, in fact at our club we positively encourage members to try as many partners as possible and whilst the old adage: "Try to play with someone more experienced than yourself to learn from" holds true. The experienced rude golfer can have a lot of fun showing off their skills to a novice.

There are always some players who seem to spend most of their time playing with themselves, this seems a terrible waste of time as intercourse is what our club is all about. These single players sometimes prefer to hire the services of one of our professionals for private attention than join in the cut and thrust atmosphere most members enjoy.

Course Behaviour

Foursomes are also becoming very popular. More members can be accommodated on the course at any one time and the variety of strokes seen can be stimulating to all concerned, these type of foursomes often result in a best ball competition. Foreplay is the most common activity and many a foursome ends up swapping partners on the second round.

Although most rude golfers find that playing in pairs to be their natural game, threesomes are often played. The novelty of another player can lead to an exciting open game but confusion can occur deciding who plays the hole first.

This is different from a single three ball which is very rare and somewhat of a freak of nature. The fourballs that only involve male members playing with each other is not everybody's cup of tea and many players find this alternative method of scoring a definite pain in the butt.

Unplayable Lie

The players' balls are deemed unplayable if clean contact can not be made. If, for instance your balls should be stuck in a very tight crack or wedge between two large mounds and no forward motion is possible, you may remove them without any penalty.

Hazards

Some holes have very high lips. When tucked up tightly against the front edge you can find gaining entry a problem. It is amazing how many nooks and crannies you can find when you are dug in deeply. You may feel going down on your lay is the only way to lick it.

In hot conditions play can come to a complete standstill because of a dry crack. If your balls are lodged in an arid slit and you think damage may occur, just put your finger in and hoick the thing out. Again for this type of hand relief there is no penalty.

SAFETY PLAY

With so much tackle flying about in all directions the rude golfer has a duty to keep safety in mind to stop those unwanted little accidents. A player with bad habits sometimes infects others, it is best to think of safety first rather than feel a little rash.

If you give someone in front of you a blow on the head it is always best to loosen all clothing and administer the usual prescribed arousal techniques – a flagging member can soon be back in action.

Sweaty fingers when taking hold of the covering can over lubricate the rubbers and cause them to slip off the shaft. This is a common occurrence and ribbed sheaths may give a better grip. A rake in a bunker can be very dangerous. One stray step can lead to a quick bang with an upright pole or a sharp poke with a little prick. Watch where you're walking in the rough – an opposing player or partner will be very unhappy if you accidently step on his balls. Stomping or grinding other player's balls in to the ground is considered unsportsmanlike.

MAXIMUM COVERAGE - The use of an oversized rubber on a big shaft is always wise.

ADVICE AND ASSISTANCE

This comes under Rule 8 where a player can not seek physical assistance in making his stroke from a third party unless he has full agreement from all involved. If caddies wish to steady your shaking hands on the shaft and guide the head for you, or offer protection from the elements by holding an umbrella while you are on the job, do not be surprised if objections are lodged. Of course caddies are expected to offer rubbers when entering wet or moist areas.

ARTIFICIAL AIDS

Some artificial aids are allowed, the main concessions go to female players such a short extensions and vibrators. Vibrators have been used by lady tennis players for many years and they have helped achieve many an exciting climax in their sport.

Now with new technology, vibrators are available in most size shafts. This allows the female member to bang away for hours without the usual consequences. These techniques are especially good for breaking in virgin players.

For the male member various artificial aids have been agreed by the committee, such as in very moist conditions the head may be rubbed with chalk to give a better purchase. Also a man with failing faculties may need some artificial help to continue to play to the end.

Note: Hand warmers are allowed as long as a player does not warm his balls on them, except under winter rules.

CASUAL WATER

Casual water is a temporary accumulation of liquid. It is not unusual for players to pass small pools of water on a long round.

Sometimes these puddles appear at the most inconvenient times, perhaps you may be trying to over extend your shot and you find yourself caught short. Instant relief can be obtained by lifting your balls out of the soggy patch without penalty.

HAND RELIEF

You may only clean your balls during play on two occasions. One, on your final approach before entering the hole and secondly when you are taking relief, i.e., from an unplayable lie, casual water or when coming out of a bunker or between holes. Relief can also be claimed if fluid appears when just your bodyweight causes it to rise.

COURSE OBSERVER

The Rude Golf Society has an abundance of volunteers for course observers. Players often take a rest from the arduous task of playing 18 holes and enjoy watching others wrestling their way round. Some observers are blatant and stand as close to the action as possible. Others secrete themselves in bushes and use a more "Peeping Tom" approach. These are usually looking for useful tips and often practice on their own while watching others. Observers who become vocal with grunts and groans may put off players causing them to shoot too early.

CASUAL WATER - The use of sprinklers on the green can cause a temporary accumulation of liquid and damp balls.

COURSE OBSERVATION - If you find yourself in an observing capacity only, be sure you are out of reach of the old hooker.

BAD LAYS IN THE ROUGH

There is no point complaining, if after a good spurt of play
you suddenly find yourself with a bad lay. This is all part of
the game, put on a brave face and give it your best. Sacrifices
have to be made, concentrate on the shot ahead or the face may
close up before impact. A bad lay may not be as demanding as
you think and you will have the sympathy of others without the
pressure of a good performance. After a bad lay, the good ones
will seem so much better.

UNUSUAL POSITIONS

Not all lies are played from the normal prepared surfaces,
such as the comfort of a lush fairway, firm greens, or even
the seclusion of the rough or bunkers. Some wayward players
find themselves having to experiment with the most unusual
positions, in the course of completing their play. We sometimes
see the odd muff, but good blows can be made underwater, tight
up against a tree or even suspended in the branches. The car
park also sees a lot of action. When playing out of the norm be
careful of chafing or jarring.

CHEATING

In most golf societies some cheating goes on, but in the Rude
Golf Society it has become an artform. Cheating on your partner
is considered par for the course, although lying about scoring is
seen as a facesaver, often players cheat when describing their
success on the course.

CADDIES

Caddies are an intrinsic part of rude golf. Any member of the Society may take turns at being a caddie. Some days you may feel like being dominated by a strong player, handling their equipment, cleaning their balls or polishing their head. If you are a shy female player you may need the oral encouragement of a caddie with a silk tongue. A few lady players go out of their way to choose the cockiest and then try to cut them down to size, this is called the "Bobbit" technique.

Demanding an instant response from your caddie, telling them exactly where and when to insert his peg can give you great satisfaction.

WINTER RULES

The Rude Golf Society is not just a fair weather group of people, only ready to show off their individuality and air their differences when the sun shines. They proudly pursue their chosen game come snow or rain. Rude golfers can rise to any challenge whatever the weather. However as in most clubs during the months of November through to March special winter rules apply.

***DIVINE INTERVENTION - If you are thinking of playing a round
instead of going to work, make sure your boss doesn't catch you***

PREVENTION IS BETTER - It is wise to use an all weather cover rather than leaving your head exposed

WINTER RULES AND TIPS

In frosty conditions it is permissible to play with red balls. Some players prefer to keep their balls warm in between holes, this is allowed, but fuel driven or electrical mechanisms are not to be used (unless under strict supervision from one of the pros).

Any hanging icicles which impede entry to a hole can be removed without penalty.

Violent thrashing about in the snow with a wood is only permissable outside the sauna.

When not actually swinging, covers should be put on all heads, these are available in the pro shop with the different sizes clearly marked. Any player can quickly select the right tool for the job whatever their particular needs.

Players who can boast a large handicap under normal conditions often have difficulty during the colder months, some have trouble even starting and balls often get completely lost.

You may not always play your best in the winter season, use the time to experiment with new techniques. Winter doesn't just mean snow and ice, players can find some of the wet weather ideas much better to play in than they first thought. In fact some only come on the course if there's a promise of wet play!

Chapter VII

Learning
The Game

LEARNING THE GAME

A much quoted golf saying is that it is: "The best fun you can have without taking your clothes off" – the Rude Golf Society can better that!

Our game is played with so much enthusiasm by our members that enforced rest periods are needed by newcomers, even nine holes can be a strain to those with little stamina.

When taking up rude golf go and see an old pro and show what you have to offer. The pros are the best judge of performance, they may suggest some private lessons to build up your confidence. The last thing you want is everyone laughing at your equipment or not being able to measure up to a partner's expectations. No matter how inadequate you may feel at the start, with a good pro giving you oral, and hands-on, experience, you will soon rise to the occasion.

Now is the time to broaden your mind, relax and let it come naturally, giving and receiving are all part of learning the game.

THE BRASSIE

This is an old fashioned term for a good, wide driver, or in most cases, hooker. It has always related to something substantial to get hold of, a fat rounded body that makes you sweat when trying to lift it above your shoulders. But you are always guaranteed a good shot with so much weight to swing with.

FIRST STROKES - Not all advice should be taken to heart. Some players get by with a short back swing and a little follow through.

These days the old brassie is a rarity on the course, most players like to tuck them away out of sight and bring them on when they need solace. Perhaps after a bad lay or being away from the play for a while. Although not in the peak of condition it always makes you feel good to caress one of these well rounded globes that has seen so much action.

COURSE PRO / PERSONAL SERVICES

We have covered the role of the course pro in other chapters, how she brings players on, assesses virgins, coaxes new comers, satisfies the rabbits and runs a team of male and female assistants. Of course the pro shop is the hub of her operations, selling essential aids to help you get maximum satisfaction from playing around. Here, personal services are available from her capable team.

When joining the Rude Golf Society inauguration sessions are run by the course pro. Ladies are often seen to by a visiting male pro, as first impressions count, they usually try to suck up to him straight away. Some of the male pros can be rigid in their approach to first timers, and these ladies may not be able to take it all in, but after a visit to the bar to loosen up and get a little lubricated they find it easier the second time and just slip right in.

As for the men, they are given our illustrated book of rules and positions, this usually helps to get them in the swing. Then they are inspected by the pros for grip and stance. Posture is very important and any droopiness is corrected. This is certainly the right place for a hump, the qualified team will have you standing straight as a poker in no time.

BOOBS / MUFFS / STIFFIES

At the outset of any learning process you are bound to make a lot of mistakes. It is only natural for a novice not to want to show her boobs off to the world, or be on the tee with players watching and be far too tight to get any length, ending up with everybody trying to correct her muff. It may be that in other games no one could hold a candle to her, but having to perform and gyrate in front of others could mean shedding her old habits.

We do arrange private lessons for girls who are used to playing with themselves. These are organised at Mossy Hollow by our head tutor Master Bator.

For the new male members who join in the pro's group activities, that first hand shake in the pro shop with a mixed audience may make you go rigid or completely wilt. It may be best to go to the practice facilities first and crank yourself up.

After a few minutes you may feel a little stiff. Just go to the club massage area and see the masseuses or the relief manageress, after a quick rub you will soon spurt into action.

RHYTHM METHOD - Swinging with a predictable action is one way of playing around, but remember one slight miscue and you may come off the shot.

RHYTHM METHOD

Safety is paramount in the Rude Golf Society and the committee are almost religious in their fervour to promote it. Some players who have a very catholic taste in sport still have no conception. They tend to live very dangerously when swinging, leaving the out come of their play up to the rhythm of their shaft and being able to pull their shot. This method is not highly recommended as a mistimed stroke can make you come off the shot, or pulling out at the last second can leave you with a messy snatch.

QUICK HOOKS

There are players who when playing around find their partners slow and lethargic. This can lead to a lack of concentration, followed by the tendency to have a quick hook. After being sucked to the left or right you may find your game perking up.

GRIPS

Grips are as varied as the game itself, what's good for you may not suit other people. Do not be afraid to experiment with new ways of holding your tool. They may feel awkward at first, or even painful, but it could be worth it. You could just get the edge by being able to squirt your balls a little bit further. Perseverence is what is needed, do not eject it after only a few tugs of the wrist.

THE COURSE PRO IS AN EXPERT IN GRIPPING SHAFTS, HERE ARE A FEW SHE USES WITH OUR MEMBERS:

THE ORTHODOX GRIP

Used by most of our members when they are on top of their game. By placing both hands around the object, sometimes overlapping the fingers to get even more purchase, a strong and reliable grip can be held. The confidence to be gained means that bodyweight between the elbows and feet can be held in perfect balance even during the most powerful strokes.

THE "V" GRIP

Making the "V" sign is a sure way to let other players know you are in control of your game, it can mean that other partners are not needed, you want to play with yourself.

BASEBALL GRIP

A useful grip for members with small hands, very popular with lady players whose fingers do not comfortably encircle the thicker shafts. Using the baseball grip in a positive way can lead to a smoother, quicker, fluid delivery.

OVERHAND GRIP

Some players find they have more control on shorter strokes if they adopt an overhand grip. Trying to make a difficult approach whilst looking over a couple of large mounds can make a player require a gentle touch with more feel.

THE HOOKER'S GRIP

A grip often advised by our course pro when a member's bad habits need correction. A firm hand is needed to stop the violent swinging of the balls as they hang in the air.

THE PROFESSIONALS GRIP - Our course pros practice their grips religiously.

GRIP TIPS

Plant one hand firmly on the shaft, then slowly slide the other onto the fleshy butt in front of it. Moisture can get on your fingers when making your grip. If your shaft has a rubber covering be careful no slipping occurs when making strokes. Unwanted accidents have been known to happen.

CARE OF EQUIPMENT

Learning to take care of your equipment is one of the first lessons in rude golf. Your tools can only take so much humping and bumping around, if you do not look after them you will end up having them strapped up or worse.

Cleaning and oiling the head is essential, if you just leave it for weeks they will start to smell like old fish and need a damn good scrubbing.

You should also clean up after entering each hole, as you don't know what has been there before you. Players who have poxy habits and use dirty equipment can contaminate their partners and the pro ends up with a dose of members at her clinic.

SEEING THE BALL

Most members of the Rude Golf Society have little inhibitions, some take immense pleasure in displaying their tackle to others. Our female players rarely turn a hair at a male member with a hand full of balls. Unfortunately some novices, virgins, and players of a nervous disposition can be off in a flash. This may leave the extrovert member feeling very exposed.

PLAYING INTO THE WIND

There is always some old fart at any club who gases all the way round, making air shots and dropping one every now and again. Without any consideration he will grunt his way up and down the fairways slowing up play or putting others off completely.

You can often find a severe blockage at the rear of such players, but no one is keen to play through. It needs a player with an iron will and be slightly unhinged to advance. Playing into the wind is always a disadvantage, one has to steel oneself against the smell of defeat. Make sure you hit as hard as possible to be sure of striking the target, this is when you will find a plugged ball a great advantage.

PRACTICE GROUND

This is a popular part of the course widely used by all members and presided over by our professional Rusty Crack and her capable team of assistant pros.

All types of problem can be cured with systematic practice, a few hours with a pro can give you years of pleasure on the

course trying out the new techniques learnt.
New members can often be a little shy when having to perform in such a public arena, preferring to watch than join in. Our pros can soon invite them to be on the inside, putting out the most friendly of warm welcomes.

Enthusiastic new members can be found from dawn onwards trying to cure their problems. Our German professional, Flopsie Tyttenhanger, likes to take these "early comers" in hand personally. These members are usually inexperienced and tend to get over-excited at even the sight of the first hole. This poor technique can lead to disappointment for all concerned. Whilst spending an hour with undivided pro attention can seem exciting in itself, "coming too early" is a habit that needs curing. Early comers can find themselves spending much of their time watching others.

PRACTISING AT HOME

1. *Practice in front of a mirror.*
2. *Grip the shaft lightly at first, then with a firm yet comfortable grip.*
3. *Look down at your hands on the shaft, everything O.K? . . . you're ready to play.*
4. *Move the shaft slowly back and forwards, feel the weight of the head swinging and build up the speed to a full stroke with a rhythmic action that will become fluid.*
5. *Stop when it becomes sore.*
6. *Be careful. Sweaty fingers can sometimes slip on the rubber.*
7. *However good the practice, the real thing is always better.*
8. *If it feels good you're probably doing it right.*

EXCESSIVE PRACTICE *- Too many practice strokes can sap your energy and leave you flagging when you are trying to get up the fairway.*

DISLAYING YOUR EQUIPMENT -Letting Your partner inspect your shaft and balls may reassure them, on the other hand, small pegs are best kept as a surprise.

89

Many players like to practice alone when they are away from the course. Hours after a lesson, at home by yourself, is a good time to think about the pro's points. By taking themselves in hand for a quiet hour's exercise a rude golfer can keep fit for the job. However if a satisfactory conclusion to home practice cannot be reached our pros have a free "Talk You Through It" telephone service.

"Are you standing in front of the mirror? Ready for some exercise? Today let's try the one-handed swing to strengthen up your weaker left hand. Take the shaft lightly at first in the fingers of your left hand, don't worry if it feels awkward, just move the grip along the shaft gently squeezing till you get the right 'feel'. Lift the head slightly, waggle it a few times, feels good? You bet it does. Careful does it, build up the action back and forwards.

Faster and faster, when the head feels light you're doing it right.
Before you know it you'll have a fluid delivery . . . remember to stop before you get sore."

Chapter VIII

SCORING

KNOWING THE SCORE

This is a very important part of any game of golf but in the Rude Golf Society it is almost a religion. The number of strokes taken count for very little in our game, although an excessive number taken while warming up may impede your performance when play actually starts.

Many of our members take from dawn to dusk to hump their equipment up and down the various fairways trying to complete 18 holes. The general rule of least number of strokes is best, does not apply to the game of rude golf. Players are judged on quality of play and a satisfying shot.

Too few strokes and holing out prematurely may leave your partner having to finish off the hole playing solo. The Rude Golf Society also encourages inventiveness during play although doing a whole round in 69 may be more than most members can lick.

After the completion of each hole players must mark each other's scorecards. This can sometimes lead to disagreements on under-marking and there is normally a course observer on hand for a second opinion. Their oral intervention usually satisfies everyone. If you are a virgin player don't worry about a high score, just relax and try and take advantage of a more experienced member. Always remember to start with a smaller tool, rather than a large shaft with an oversized head as novices tend to have a short snatch and can't manage the follow through.

LAME DUCK - Experience counts for a lot in this game, what you may consider a good round may be well below par for others.

Par

Each hole is scored on an individual basis, what you may consider par for the course may not be acceptable play to others. It is important to get the ground rules out of the way before play starts, always check on what areas are out of bounds.

If group play is involved, indicate which hole you are playing and try not to stray on to another fairway while it is in use.

When playing around with a partner, threesomes or foursomes safety play is very important. Leave your balls where they are, don't even think of getting your peg out until all necessary precautions are taken and your head has a good all-weather cover on it.

Balls in Motion

It is considered bad form to try and score while another player's balls are still in motion on the same hole. The best thing to do is practice your grip and be patient, it is well known that golf can be a frustrating game. Make the best of the time and thoroughly inspect your balls for any wear and tear.

HANDICAPS

The Rude Golf Society handicap system is very popular with the majority of our members. It is administered by Rusty Crack our course pro, this duty means that she can be tied up for hours a day. She does say that overseeing the handicaps can be very restrictive, but deep down she really enjoys roping the members in and does not mind them getting on top of her now and again.

If the handicaps are worked out correctly it can lead to a very close game. Players often like to talk about the bondage that can build up in such tied games.

It is also true that if you play around with a member who is so constricted by his handicap you may end up giving him a damn good whipping. This could be mutually satisfying and you might both learn new techniques from each other.

BIRDIE, EAGLE AND ALBATROSS

Within normal golfing rules, to birdie is to achieve your final shot into the hole with one less stroke than normal. To eagle out two less strokes and albatross three fewer strokes.

The Rude Golf Society see no benefit in boasting how quickly you can come to a conclusion and move on to the next hole. The general opinion is such scoring techniques are just a load of guano.

***STRICTLY FOR THE BIRDS** - Birdies, eagles and Albatrossed, this type of scoring can often drop you in it.*

SCRATCH

The Rude Golf Society does have a small number of scratch players, but they are slowly being wheedled out. Now the pro's clinic is open every day of the week and on weekends we think there is a clearing at the end of the tunnel.

LOST BALL / BEST BALL

Losing one of your balls while playing a hole is indeed an unfortunate experience. Whilst you have everyone's sympathy life must go on. If you are able to continue you may. Alternatively you can take time to retrieve the situation. If this is the case please let others play through, there is no need to spoil everyone's day.

There is the odd occasion that a player has a choice of balls. It could be their position, appearance, or just look a much better lay. A playing partner should not be marked down simply for taking a more attractive option. You may be glad in the end as the advantage taken may be quickly gobbled up and you could still hole out first.

STROKE PLAY

Many of our members enjoy nothing more than getting to grips with their stroke play. The amount of relief that can be obtained from a hands-on experience should not be underrated. Stroke play classes are run by the chief coach, Master Bater, and his assistant in whom he is very proud, Jenny Talia, who he encourages novices and virgins to play with as often as possible.

GROSS SCORE

After a hard day's play with all the best holes behind you, all that's left is the gross score. Sometimes players are embarrassed to be seen with such large figures and are often disgusted at the state of their game. Never fear – there are no winners or losers in the Rude Golf Society. We quickly forget who came first or who is always at the bottom. Tomorrow is another day and there is still time for a stiff one and a couple of quickies at the bar before you go home.

BOGEY / DOUBLE BOGEY

The bogey and double bogey are an unfortunate part of club life. Certain members seem to spend too much time digging in around the green. To get out of trouble a little roll and a quick flick is all that is required.

DOMINATING PLAY - Strict discipline in administering the handicap system can lead to player/caddie bondage.

Chapter IX

IN THE CLUB

MEMBERSHIP

Being a member of the Rude Golf Society offers numerous openings. Many a business deal is screwed down while trying out a new shaft. There is nothing better than introducing an influential colleague to the club and getting an attractive caddie to suck up to him.

Our membership bridges all walks of life, from the big knobs of industry to the hospital workers who give small pricks. The judiciary and politicians are particularly keen on the strict discipline needed for the game and demand punishments if they transgress the rules. They say they feel the benefit of being tied to this type of sport and that they are not simply flogging a dead horse – which is just as well as the use of animals has been withdrawn by the rules committee.

Here at Mossy Hollow our vice-captain is always happy to receive new members or visiting players from associated clubs. Generally no letters of introduction are needed apart from the clubs in France. This is due to the break away movement which now requires the Rude Golf Society affiliated clubs to inspect all French letters.

The golf club is always a social place and although most of a member's time is spent in the pleasurable activity of performing out on the course the clubhouse, or 19th hole, is often the area where the real action takes place.

The club bar is where tired players head for after a gruelling 18 holes, where flagging members exaggerate the length of their best strokes, dismissing the disappointment of bad holes as not

RAISING A POINT - The clubhouse is somewhere you can relax; indulge in oral pursuits and get things off your chest.

totally their fault. Celebrations can be in order as it is a club tradition that after a hole-in-one or a first round of 69 the drinks are on you.

The bar is presided over by a series of relief managers who will attend to every need, providing all the services a member could need from a simple nibble while engaging the member in oral stimulation, to arranging a variety of social events for the club bar such as Lucky Dip, Swap Shops, and the ever popular Wheelbarrow Race Nights.

ENTRY PROCEDURES

To become a member of the Rude Golf Society you have to go through the formality of presenting yourself, with your equipment on full show, to the selection committee. It is very rare for any one to be turned down, but the tradition of letting the overseeing members inspect all shafts, heads and balls goes back to the beginning of the game.

The voting in of a new member is still done in secret, but the humiliating and degrading procedure of black balling has been stopped. This is mainly because too many applicants enjoyed it and kept on re-presenting themselves.

CLUB BAR

The club bar of Mossy Hollow is run by a series of relief managers. The steward in charge is Dr Ben Dover, a retired gynaecologist who likes to keep his hand in. The club also employs an odd job man to see to all those screwing and banging jobs that need doing although he maintains that tongue and grooving are his specialities.

***RELIEF MANAGER - The clubhouse is just the place to relieve
your frustration.***

SUSPENDED BY THE COMMITTEE - Most players accept the punishments handed out. Some even enjoy being hauled over the coals.

CHANGING ROOMS

Normally at any affiliated Rude Golf Society there is only one changing room. Here at Mossy Hollow we also have communal showers where scrubbers are supplied on demand.

PAY AND PLAY

There is a pay-and-play policy operated at all Rude Golf Society venues. This is to encourage prospective players to come as often as they like, although priority is given to existing members on all holes. The course pro, Rusty Crack, has always encouraged pay and play, in fact it is the cornerstone of her business.

EXPECTATIONS

The Rude Golf Society is all about enjoying yourself, it doesn't have to be a masochistic pursuit. You can be whoever you want to be and play any hole in your own style. Whether you play around once a year or can manage 36 holes in a day we can always find a partner or group to accommodate you.

GOLF/FLOG - We believe it is no coincidence that having a good back swing and a strong follow through are the key elements of more than one sport.

In The Club

One of our oldest female players, ex-pro Ruby Quim, has records going back 40 years to prove she has played around with everyone at Mossy Hollow, she is renowned in Rude Golf Society folklore and is our honorary open champion.

Not all society members are expected to have her enthusiasm or stamina, but the criteria for all females is to have an open attitude and a good feeling for sport. Everyone feels men's entries should be a little stiff, therefore male members are expected to be upright pillars of strength, always ready to do their duty, standing proud with heads held high.

Future Of The Society

The Rude Golf Society has tried to increase the size of its members every year and we have also increased the number of holes available. New comers are always welcome whether you are a virgin, novice or rabbit, the game of rude golf is for everyone. We are always looking for spunky new players to join us, our pros gobble up new talent as fast as it comes.

Take up the challenge to couple with our members and show us what you're made of. For membership details contact: The Mossy Hollow Golf Club.

YOUR PERSONAL INVITATION

The Outrageous 19th
cordially invites you to visit
(it would be rude not to)
'virtually' the best clubhouse,
golf humour web site and
online store orbiting
the world.

www.outrageous19th.co.uk

The site is also home to one
of the strangest, funniest
golfing groups on the planet -
The Rude Golf Society - that deliberately takes the official rules
literally – and misinterprets every single one with outrageous
double entendres.

We at the Outrageous 19th believe that our great game of golf
is the best fun you can have with your socks on (well it is if you
don't get out much or have
little imagination) – but it can
also be the most frustrating of
pursuits clothed or naked!

No matter how many times
you tell yourself it's just a
game you know when you
quadruple bogey the hole your

novice partner birdies you will want to bend your putter over their stupid fat gloating head.

All too often our golfing day is spoilt through poor shots/bad equipment/slow play/too hot/too cold/lost balls/course conditions/too wet/too dry/bad back /bad front/ … Alternatively by being hauled up by a minor official or stuffy member over a tiny infringement of some petty rule – let's face it golf can be a genuinely depressing game!

At the outrageous 19th we feel that people take themselves and their passion for golf far too seriously – if you can't laugh at yourself then you can be assured that someone else can do it for you. As ardent believers in equal opportunities we try and send up or offend all that play our revered game.

This Great British humour site plants it's tongue firmly in its cheek and looks at all that is dear to the enthusiast. We offer an alternative way of interpreting the hallowed rules and traditions – as we all know you can view things from many different

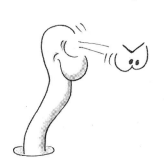 

perspectives or as the Brazilians aptly demonstrate there is always more than one way to de-fur a pussy.

The humour is in the time honoured 'saucy seaside

postcard' tradition that has caused countless titters and amused many in polite society worldwide from Little Hampton to Gobblers Knob. The gags are only as rude as you are, which means we will probably have the police round. On the other hand, if you have the mind of a Mother Superior they may just bring a gentle smile of inner pleasure to those dry withered old lips once you have powered up your appliance and logged yourself on.

The Outrageous 19th produce the most outrageous golf humour books – cards - mugs – prints and accessories – that are all put together in the best possible taste!

Our products are outrageously funny, slightly risqué, littered with innuendos, unique and all based on the golf rules and regulations that we all hold so dear as well as golfing terminology and coaching tips that every golfer will be far too familiar with.

The Outrageous 19th range is completely geared up for the £10 and under market – ideal for gifts, prizes, invitation cards - brilliant for golf days and societies or just to cheer up a bad round.

So why not take up our invitation - not only are there great golf humour products but also free downloads – e-cards - video clips and more Rude Golf Society updates than you could shake your shaft at.

Come and see what's on offer and enjoy a bloody good laugh - just log on to:

www.outrageous19th.co.uk

Remember! - You can also order any of our products from any good pro/golf shop.